Coloring book for adults and kids amazing sheep design

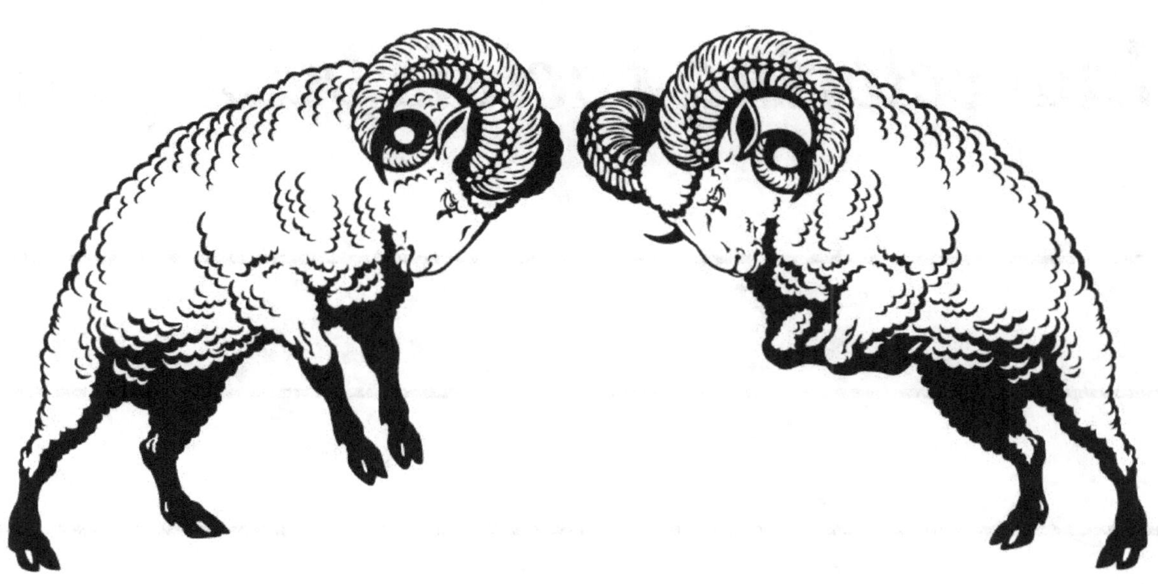

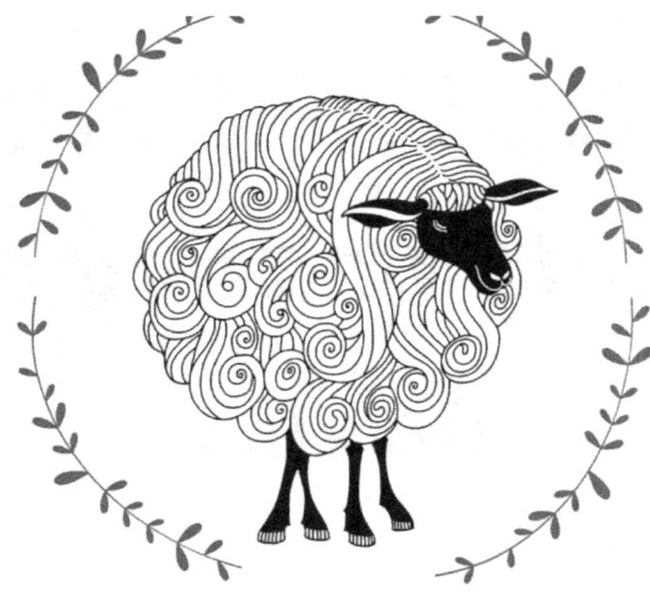

This coloring book is belongs to

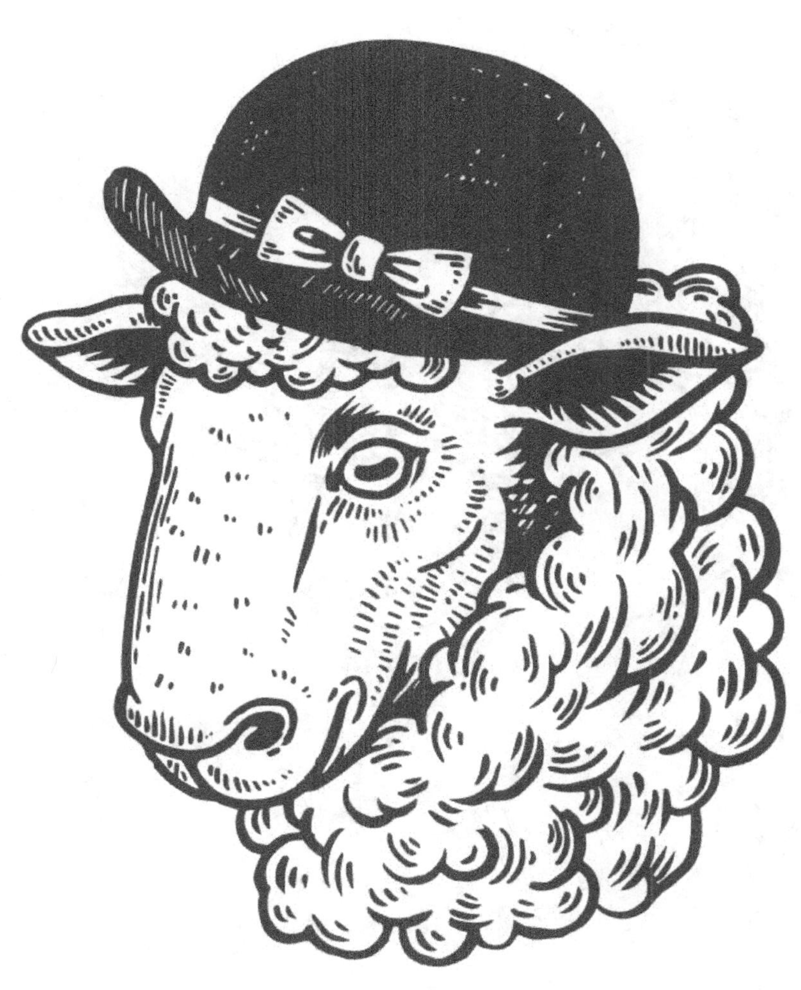

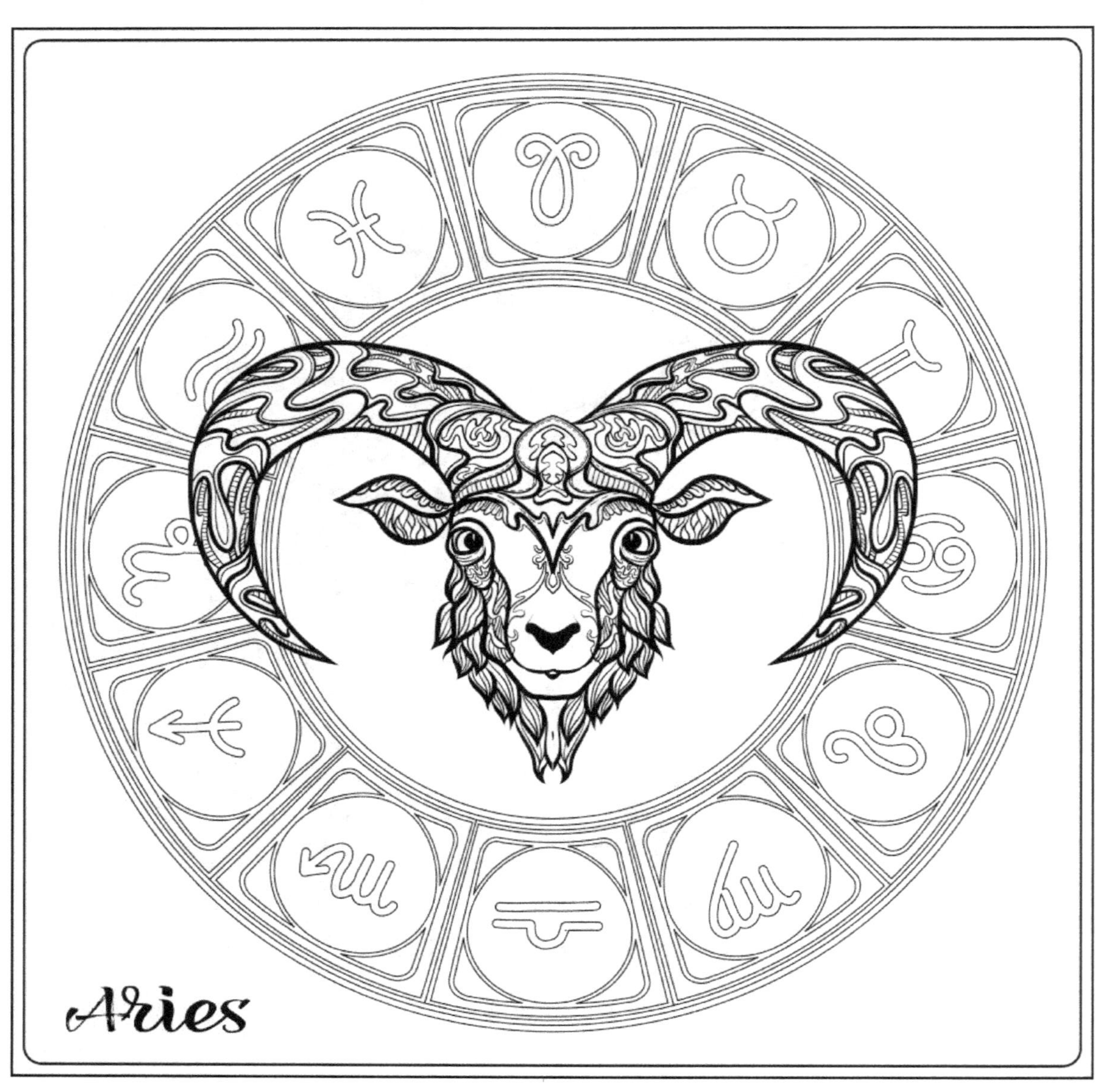

Aries

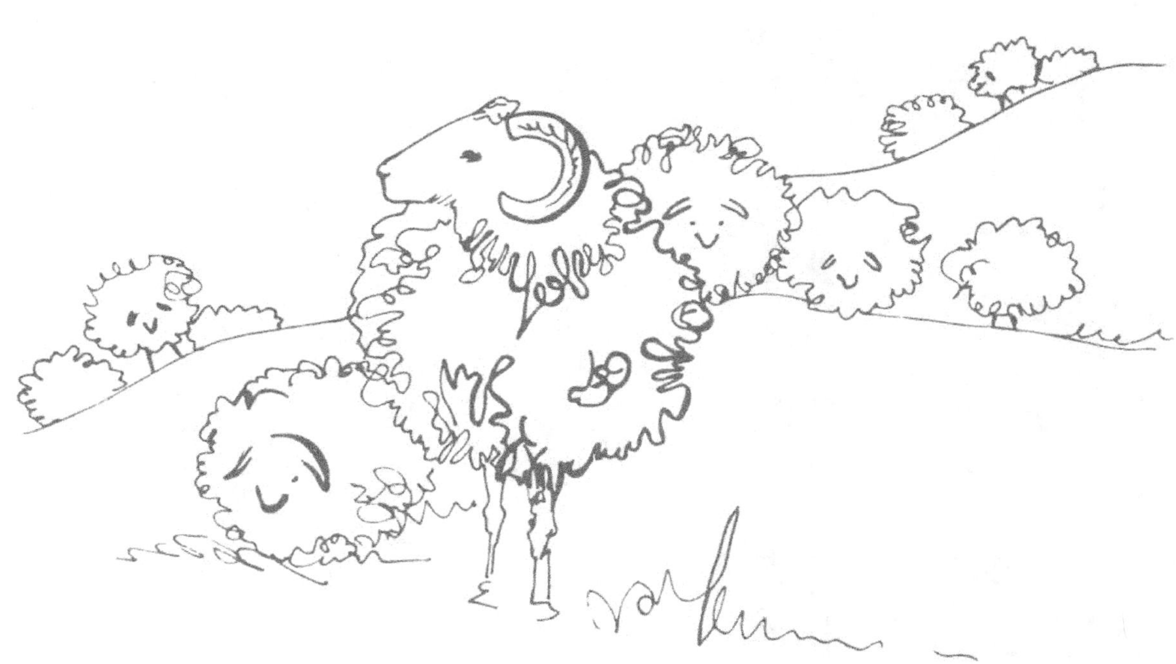

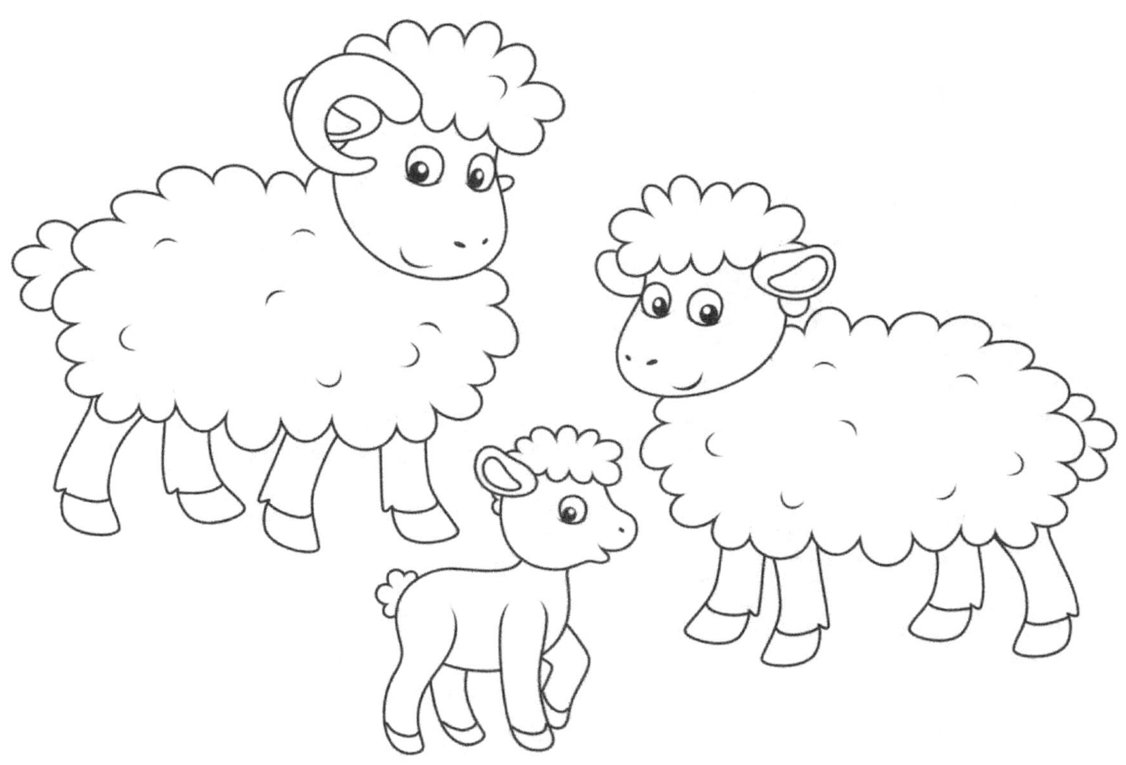

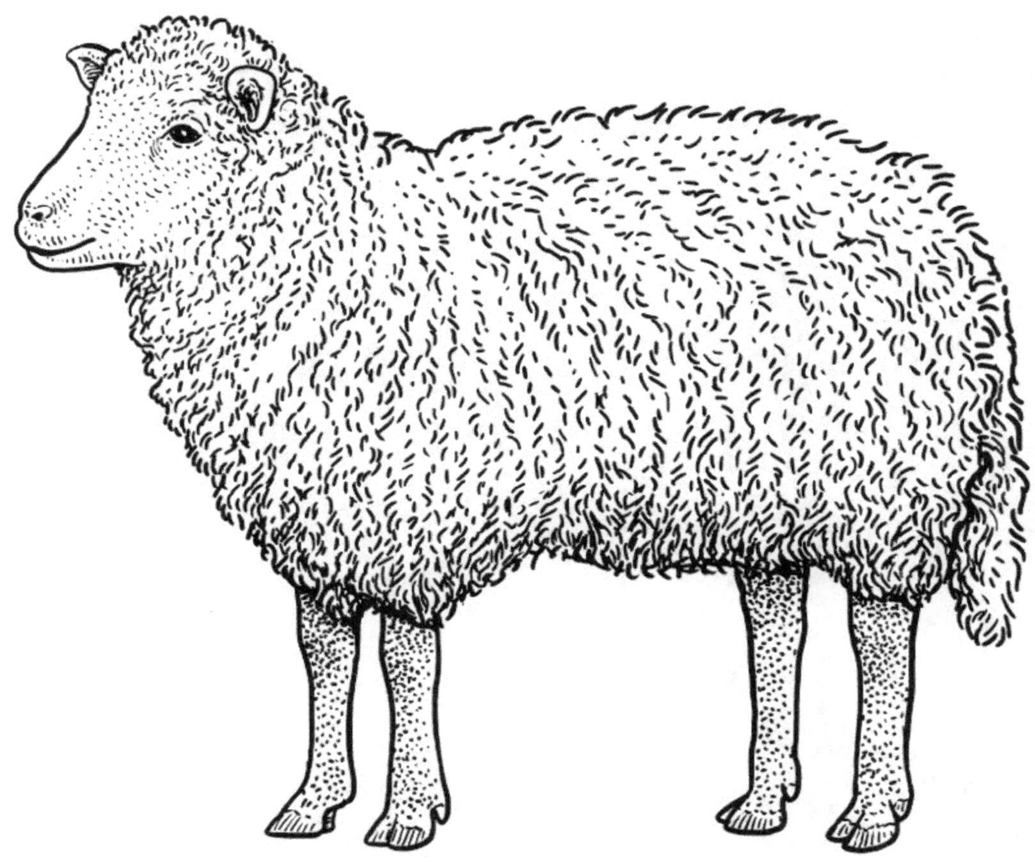

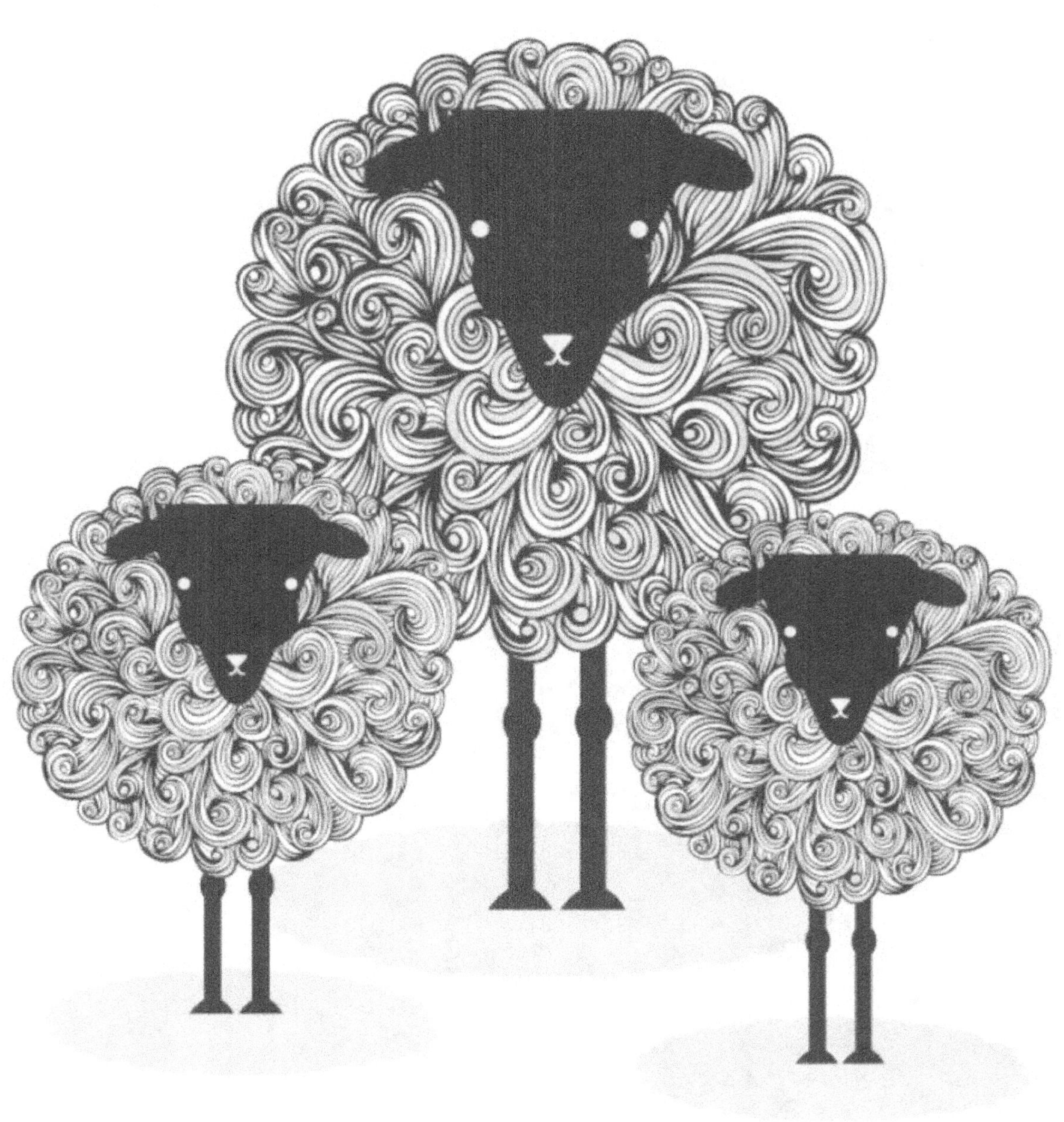

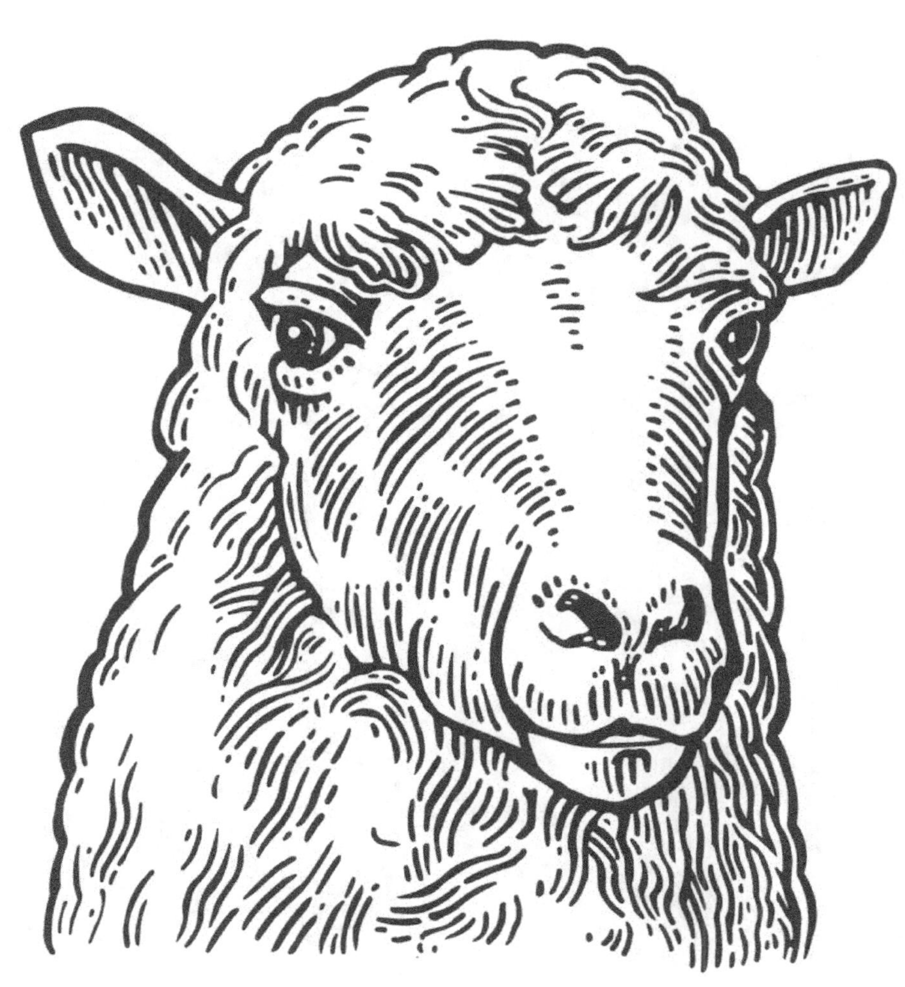

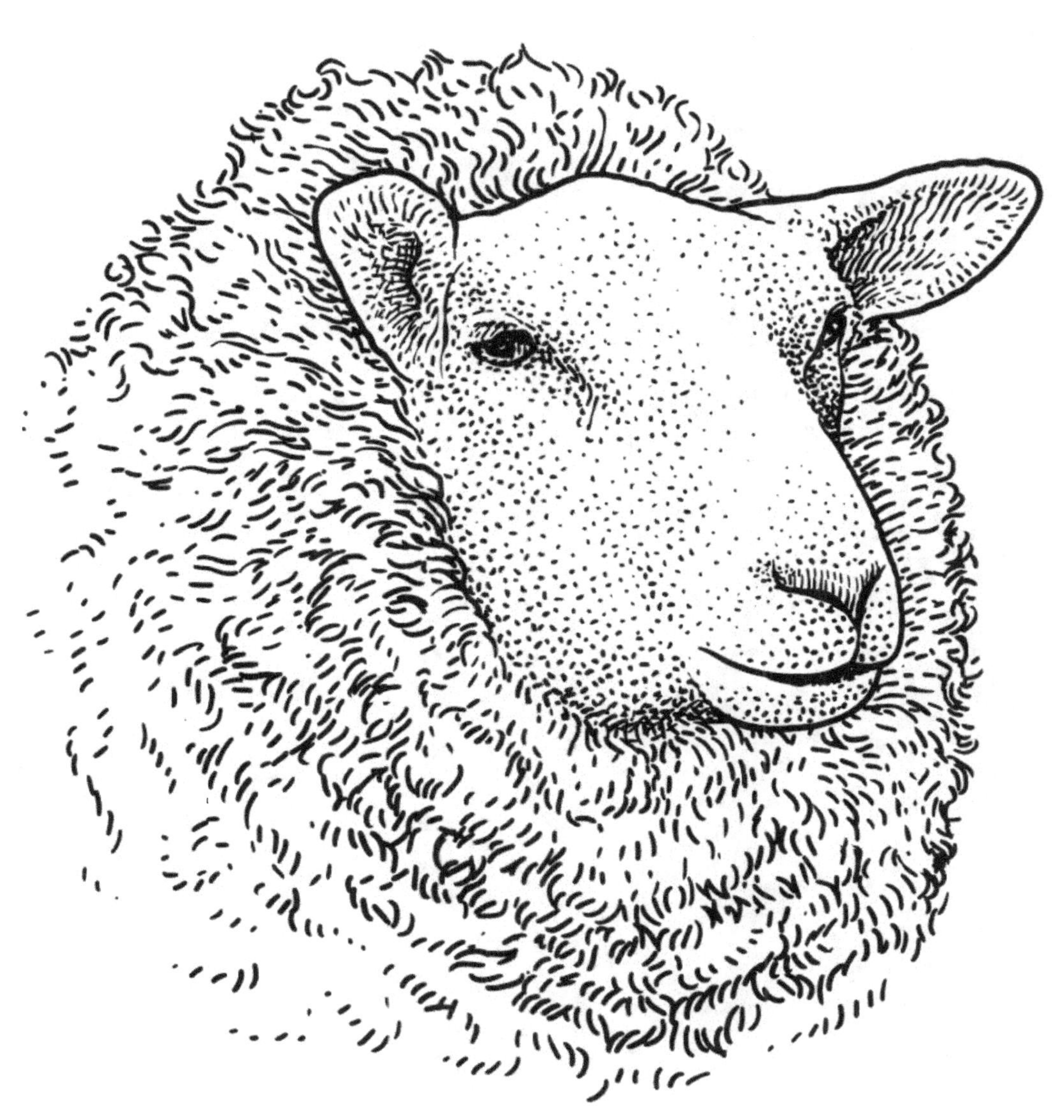

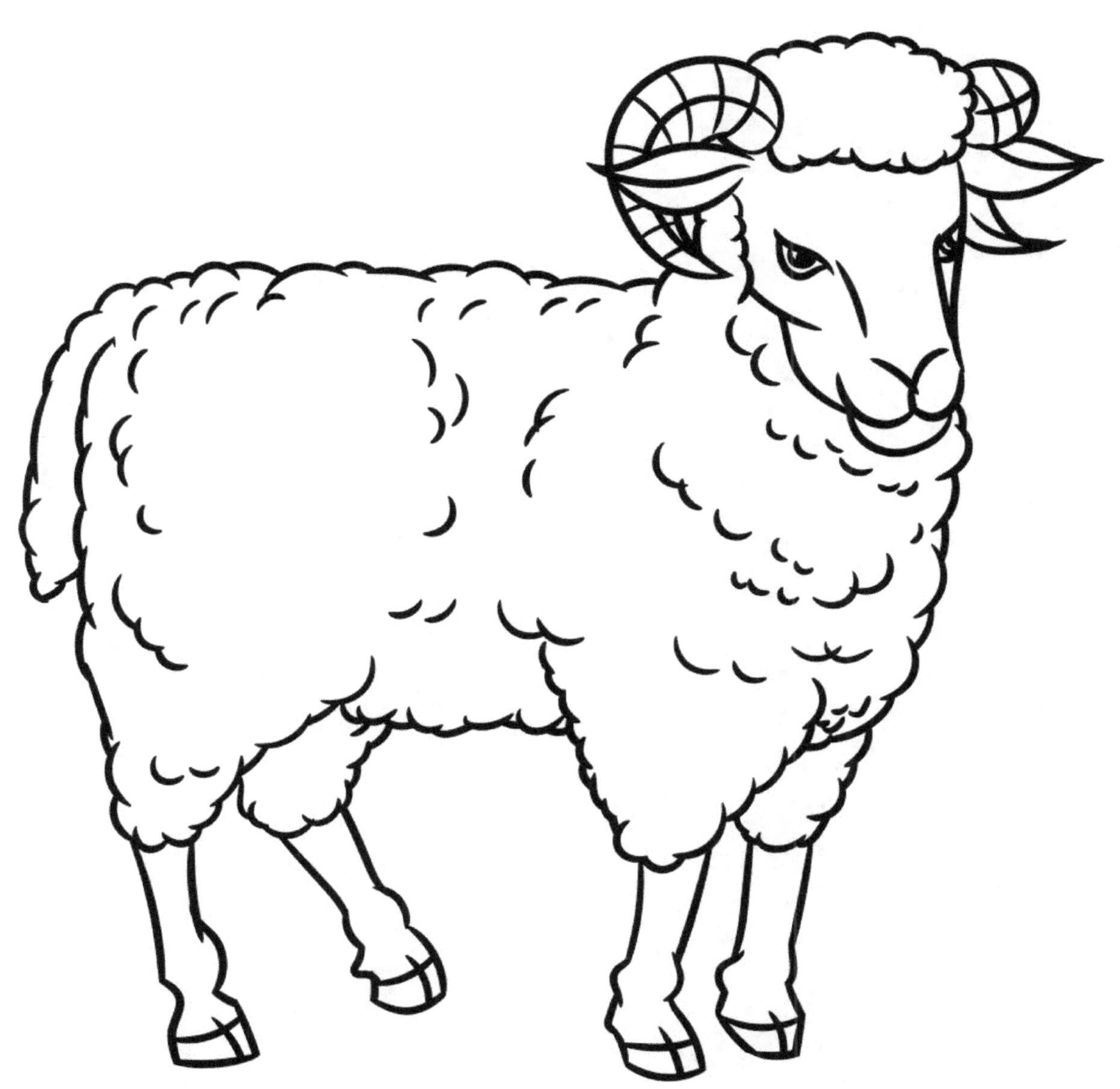

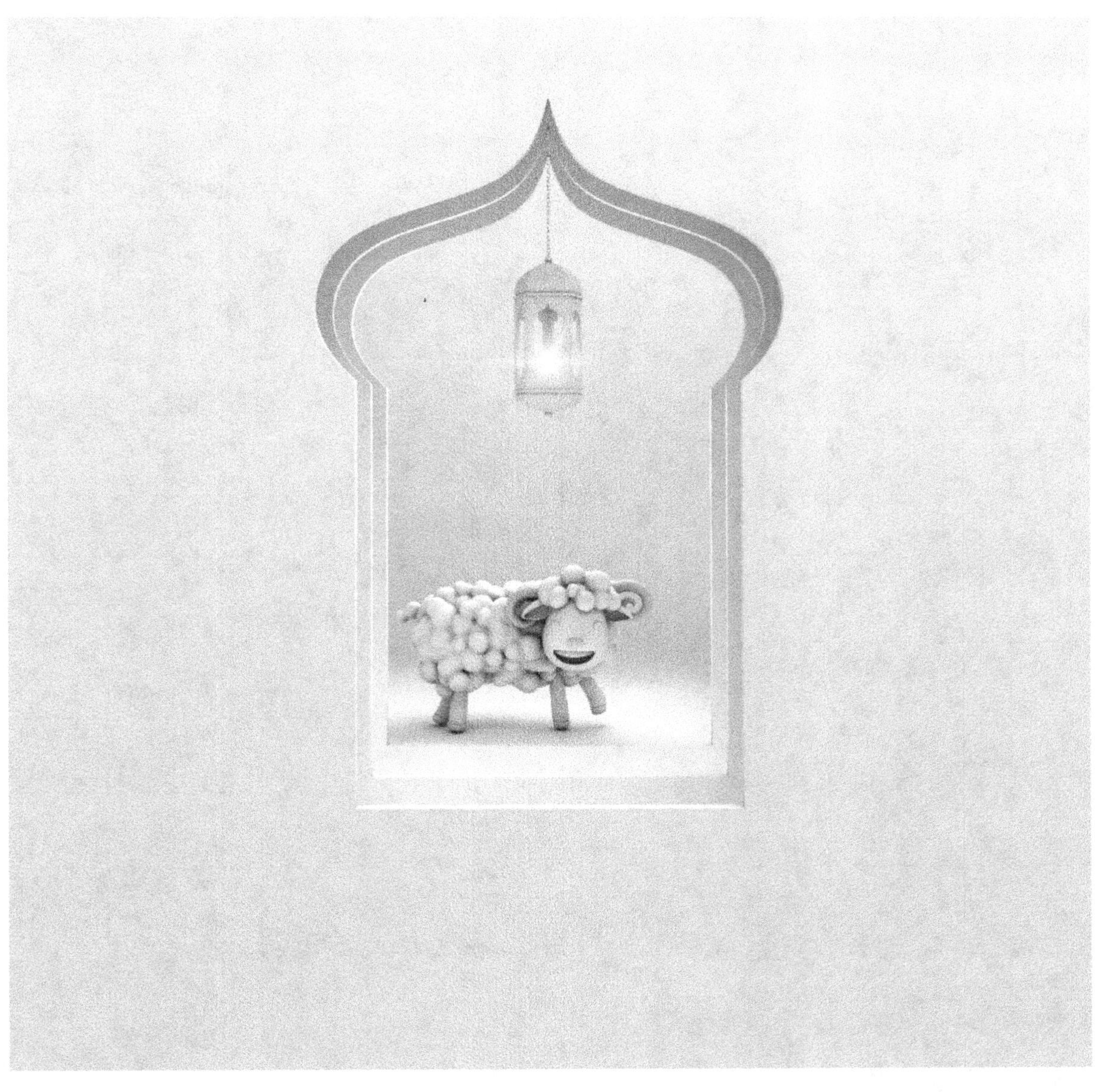

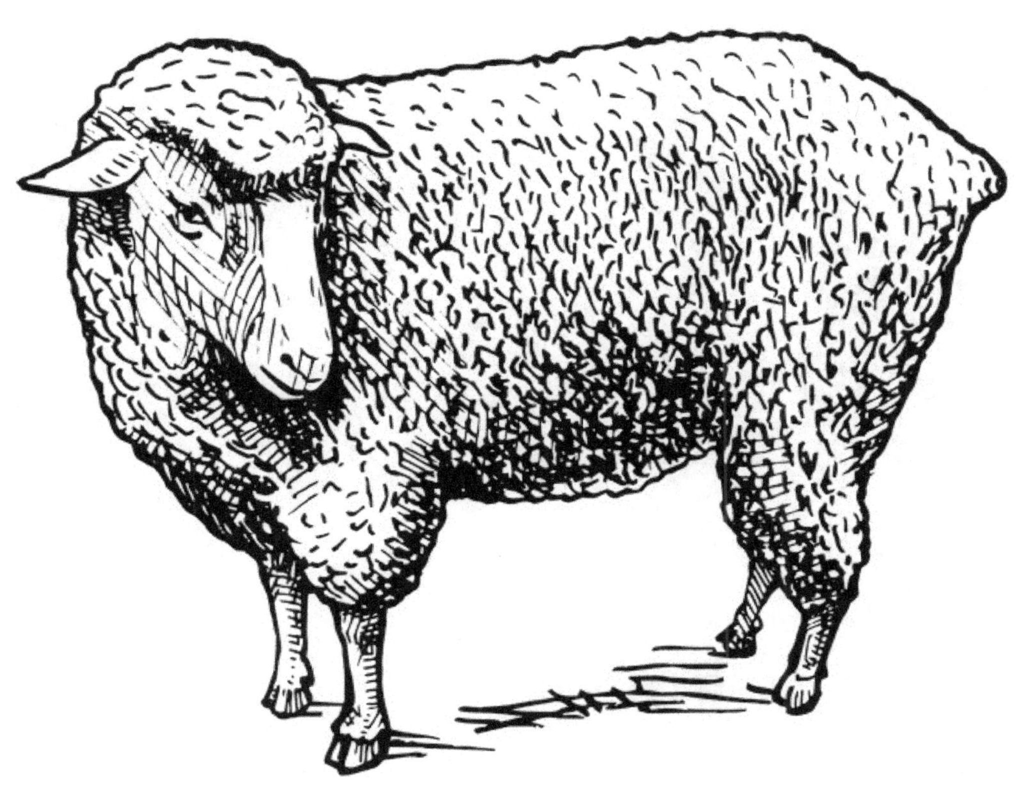

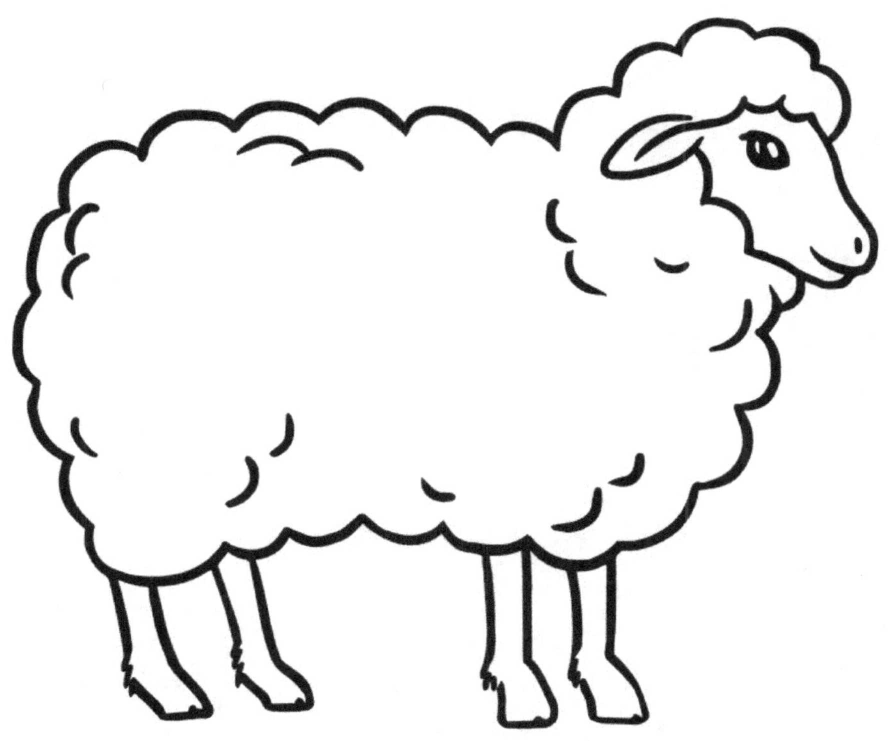

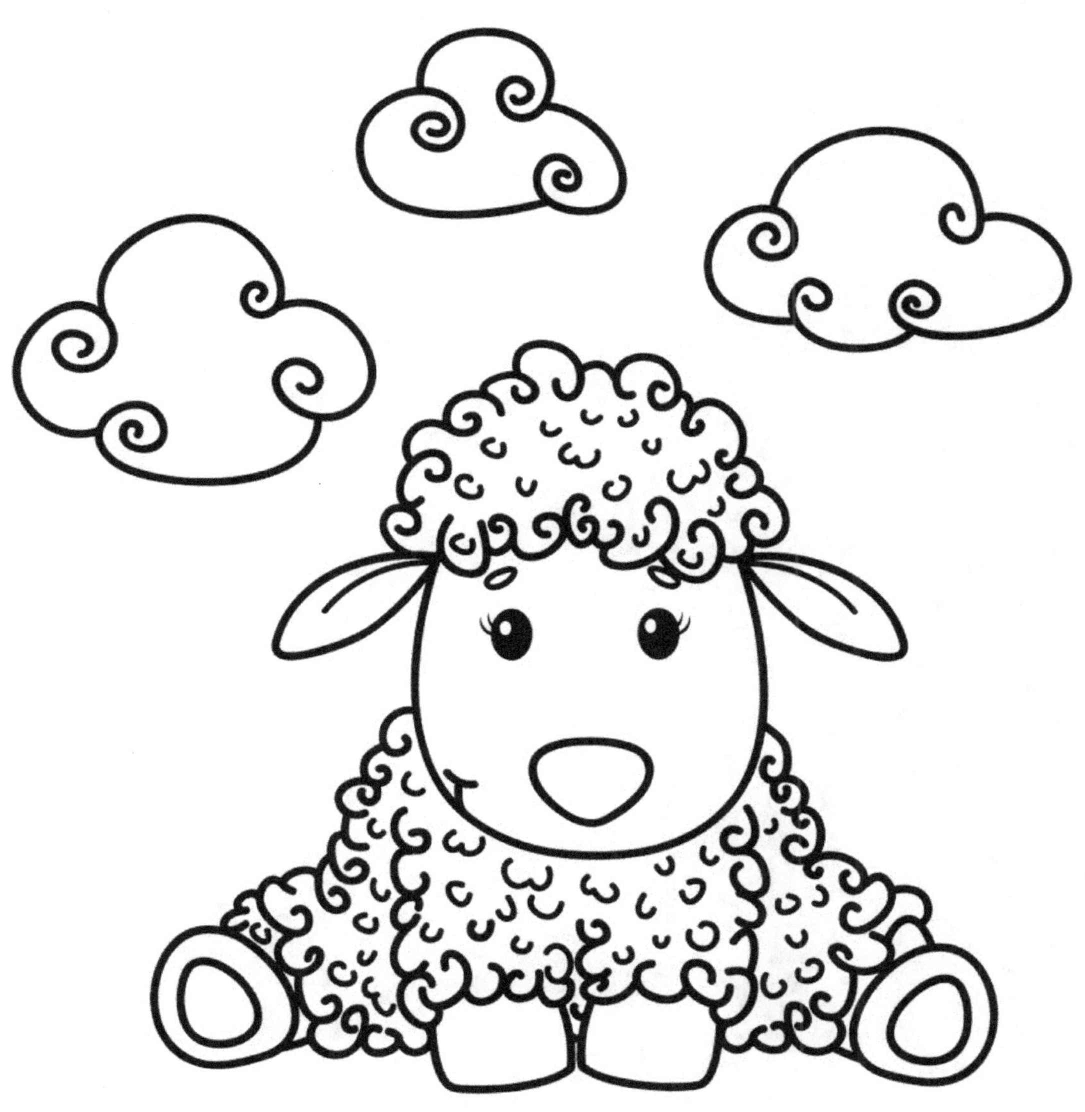

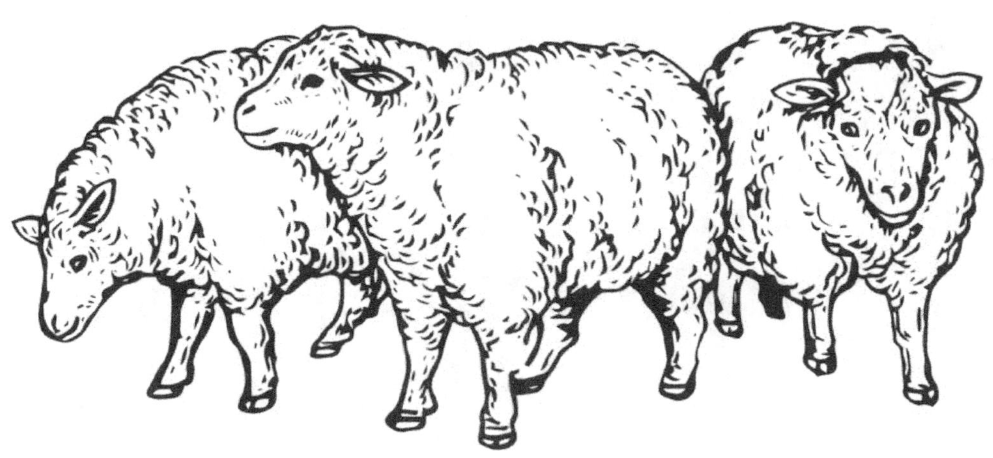

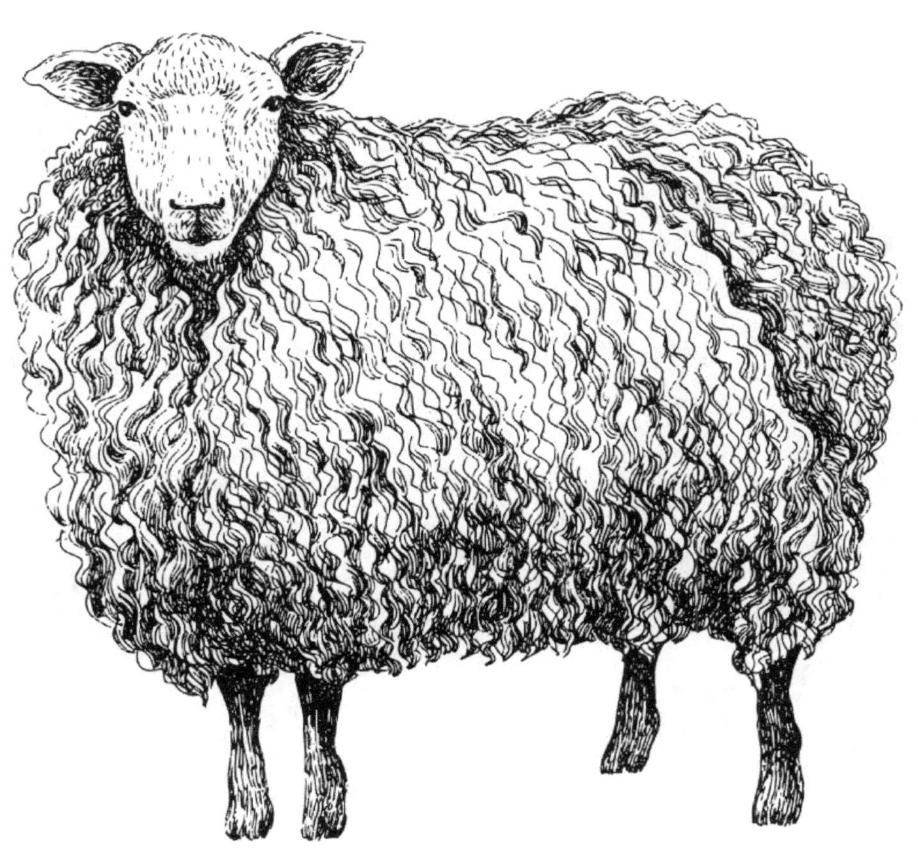

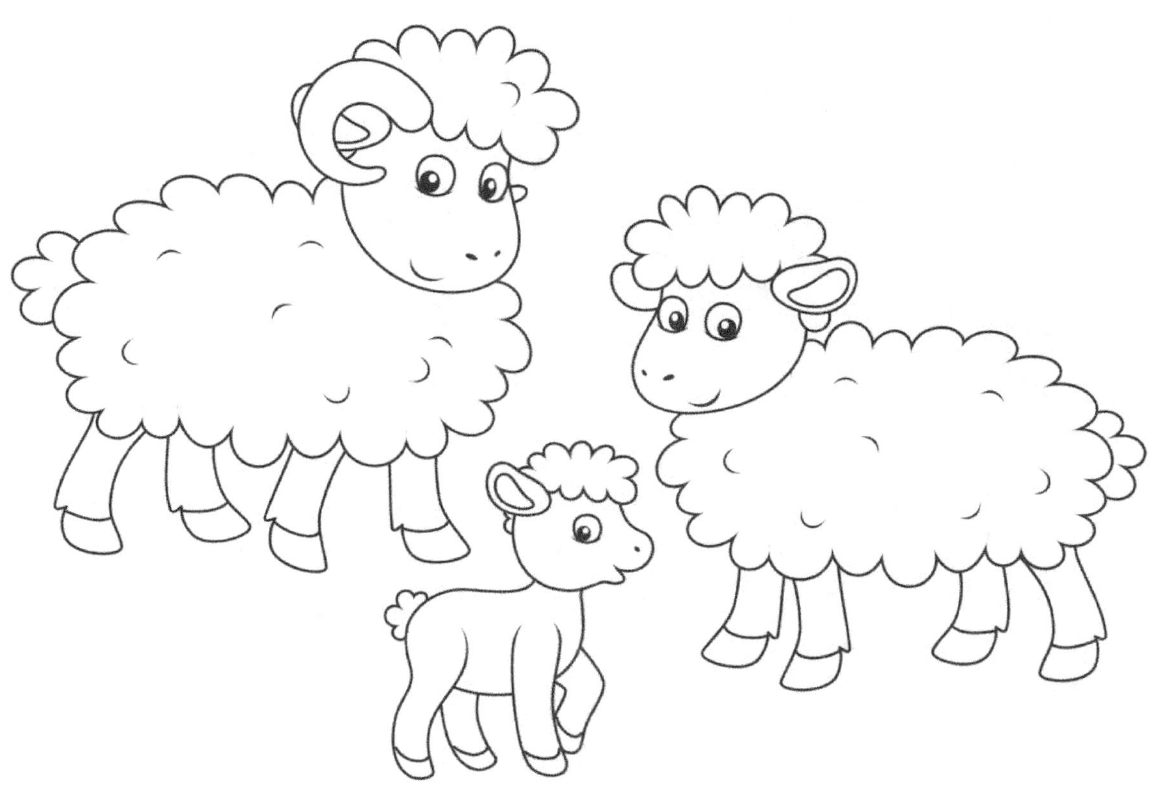

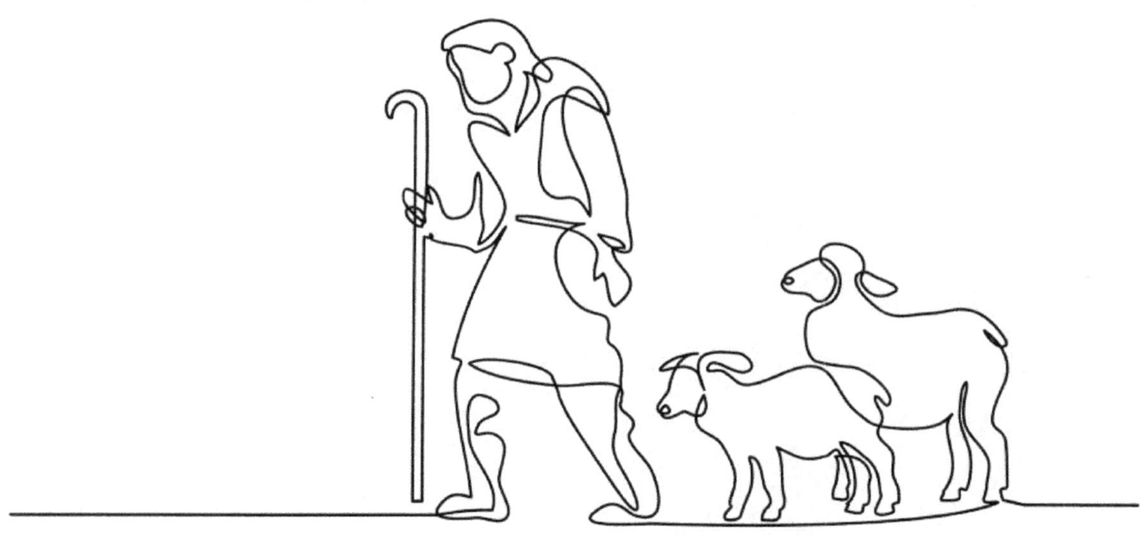

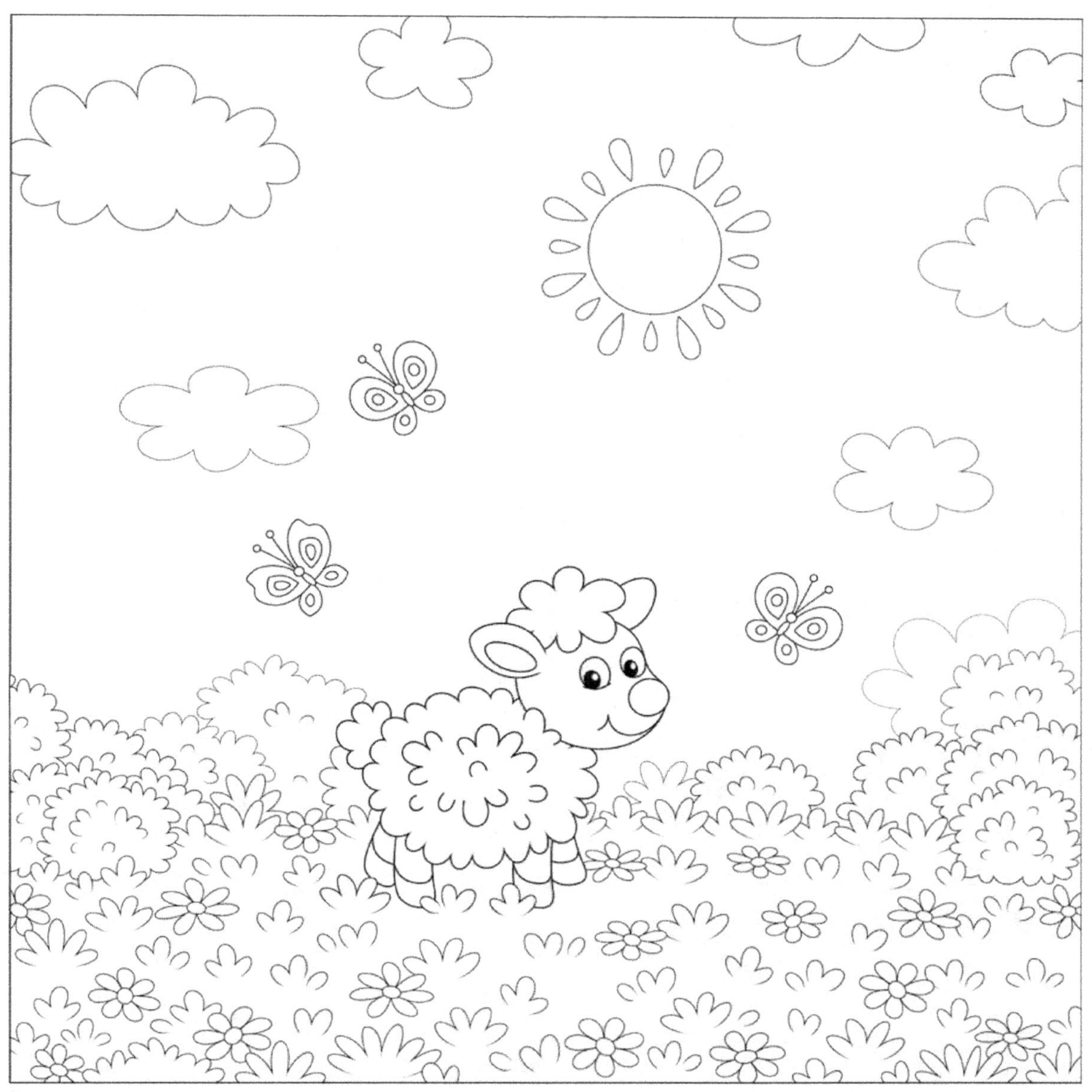

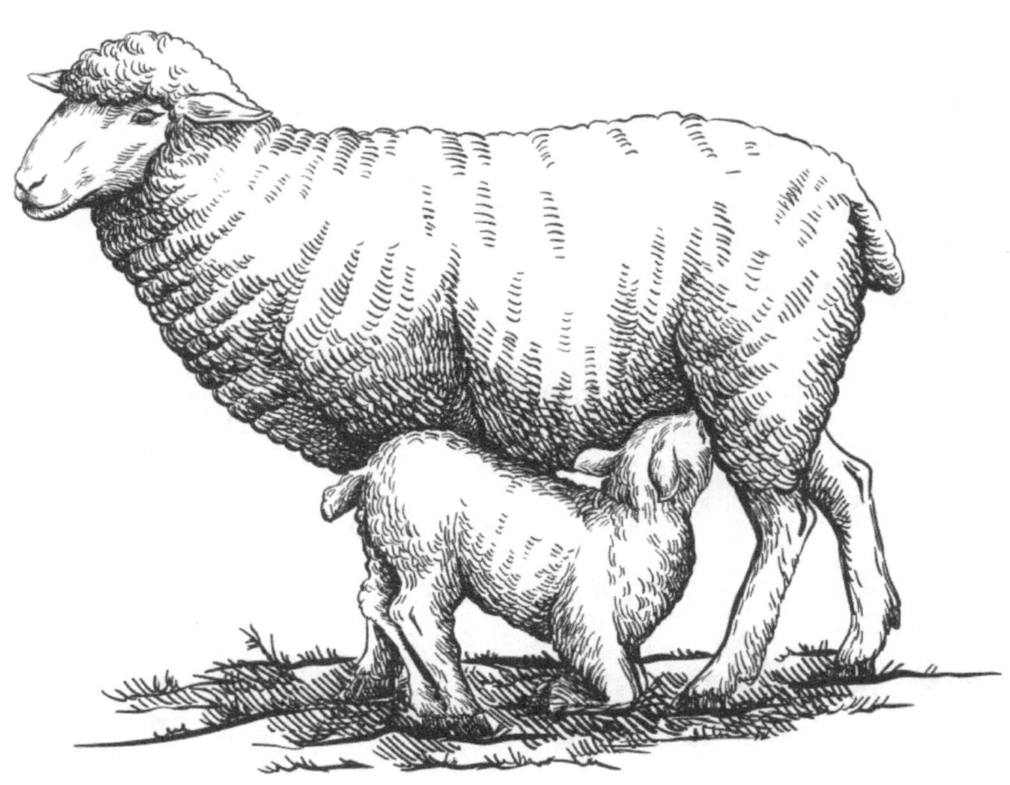

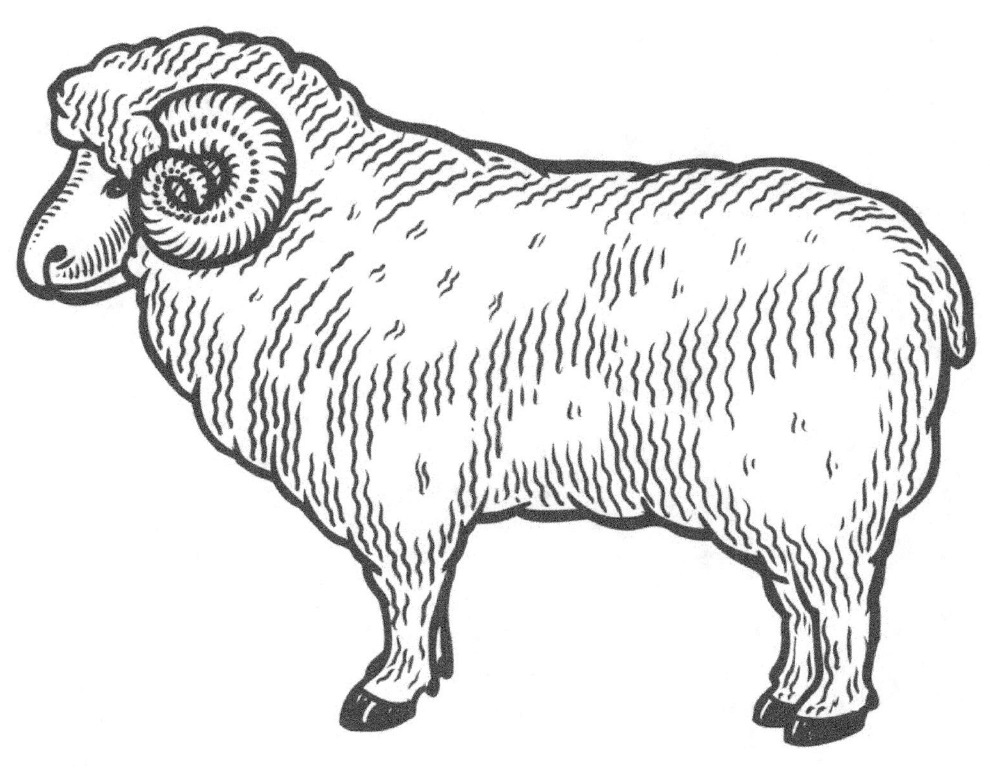

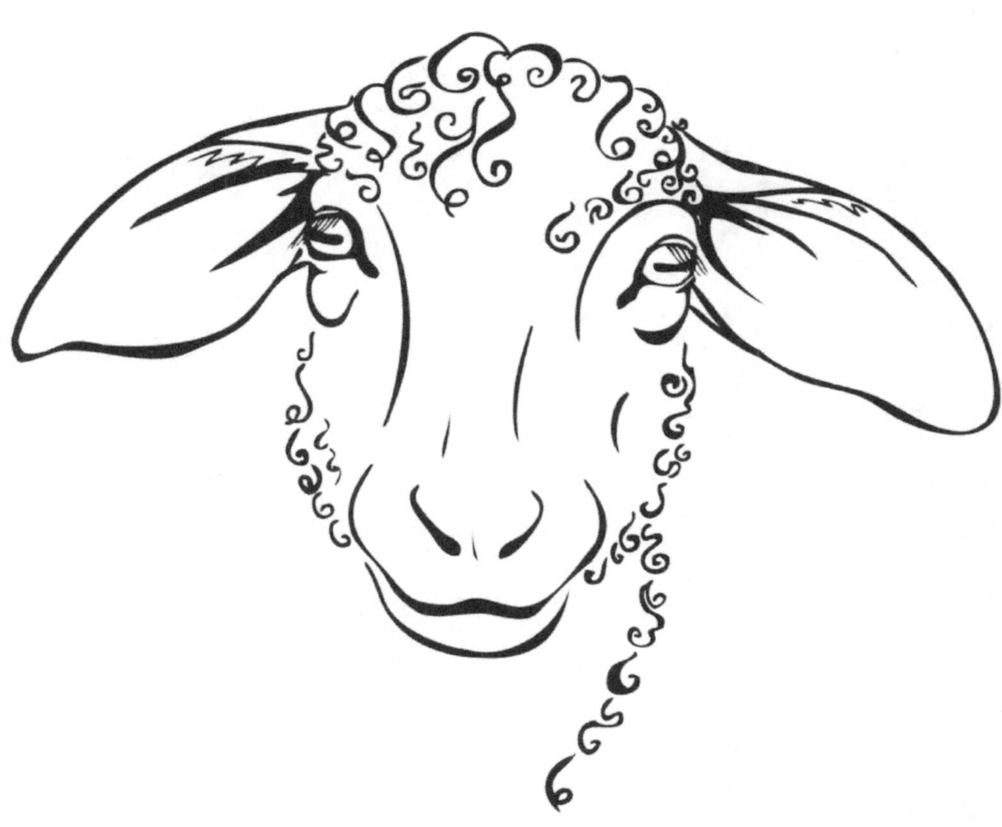

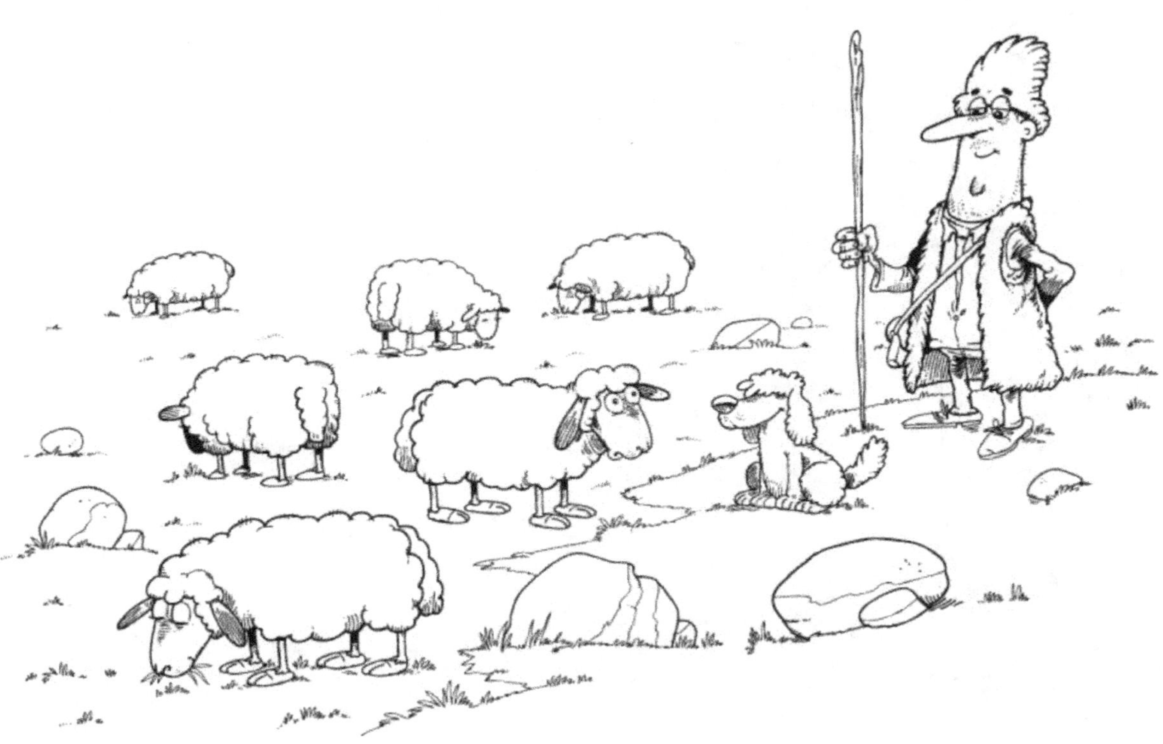

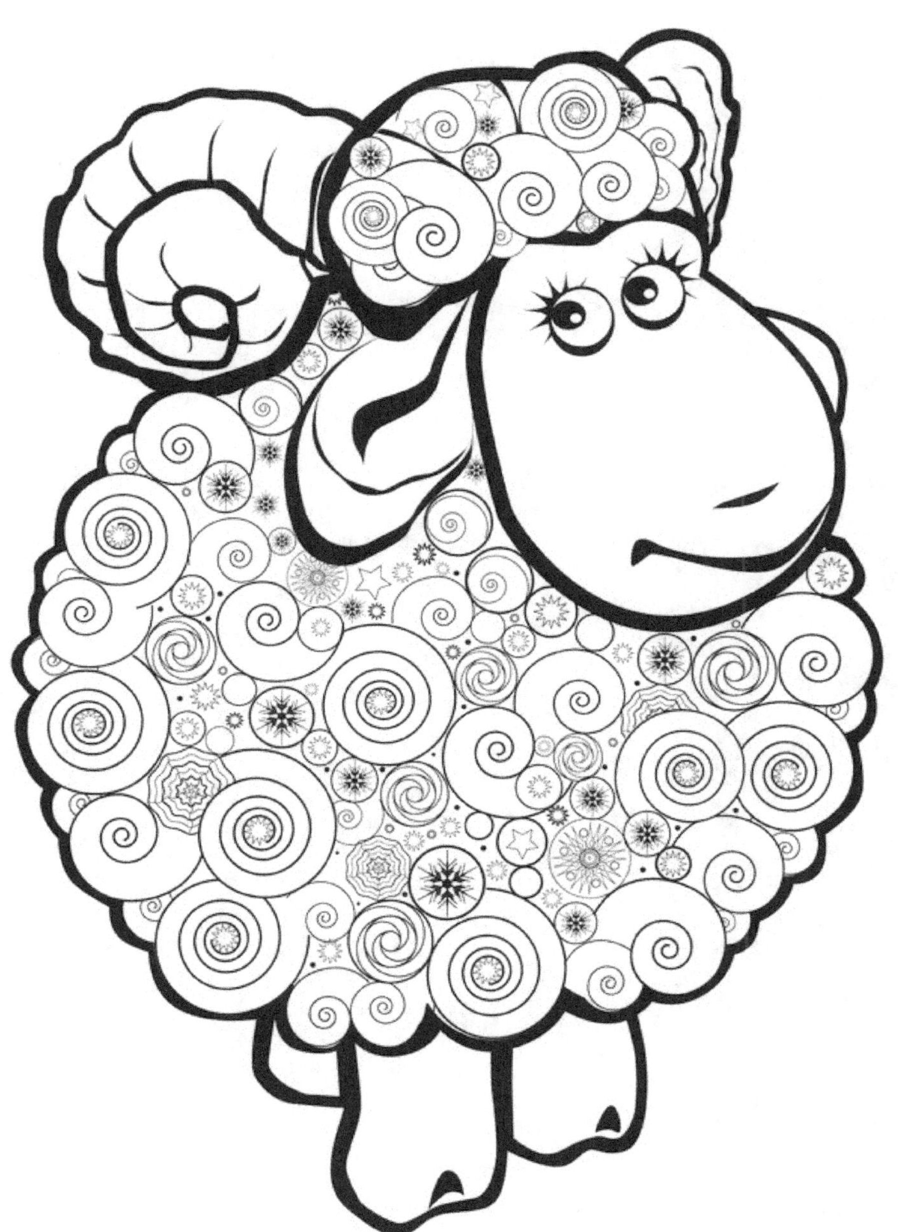

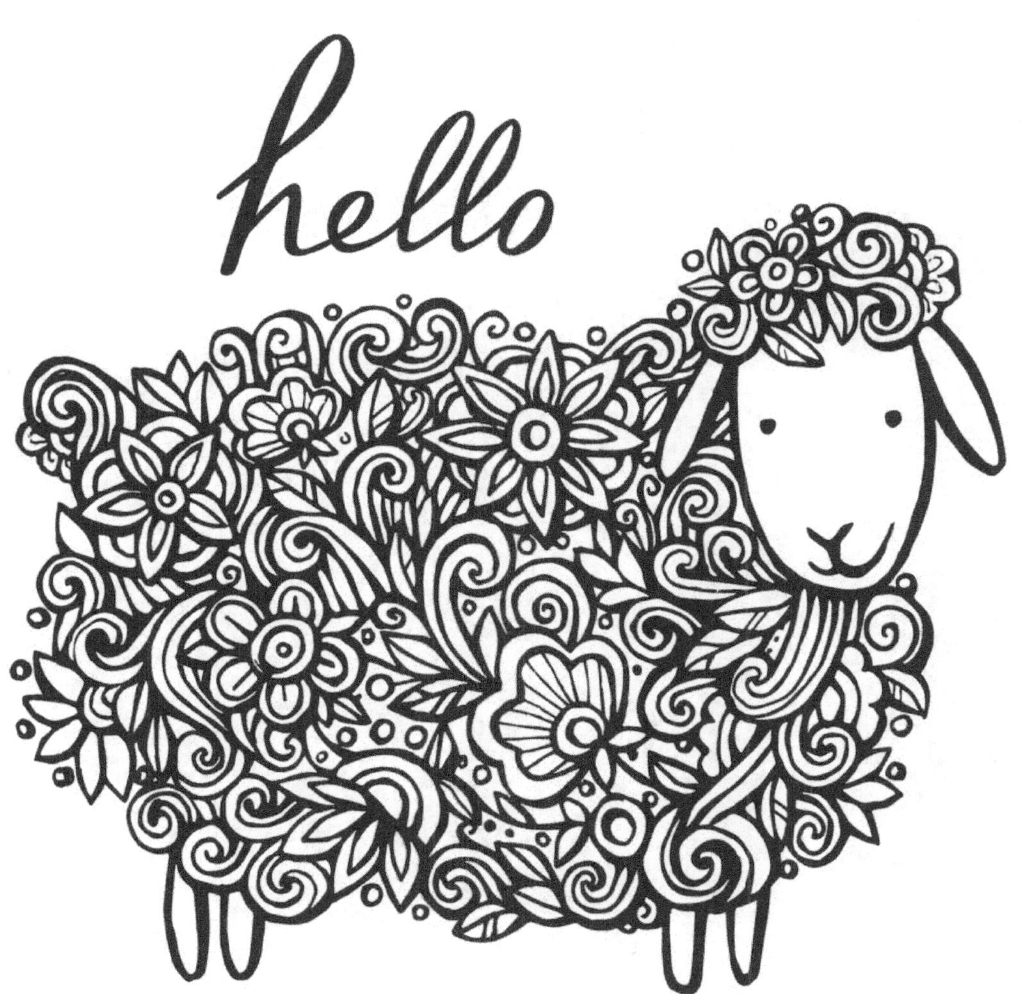

hello

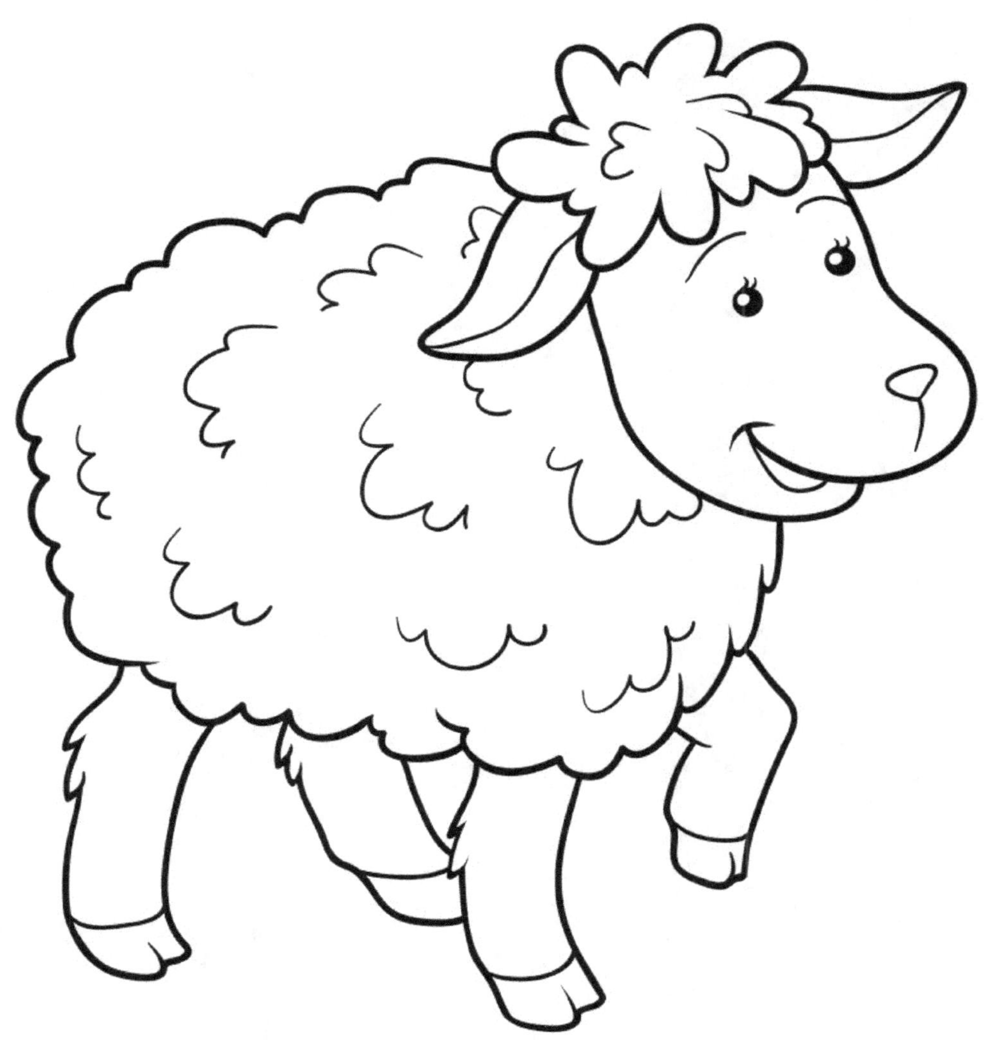

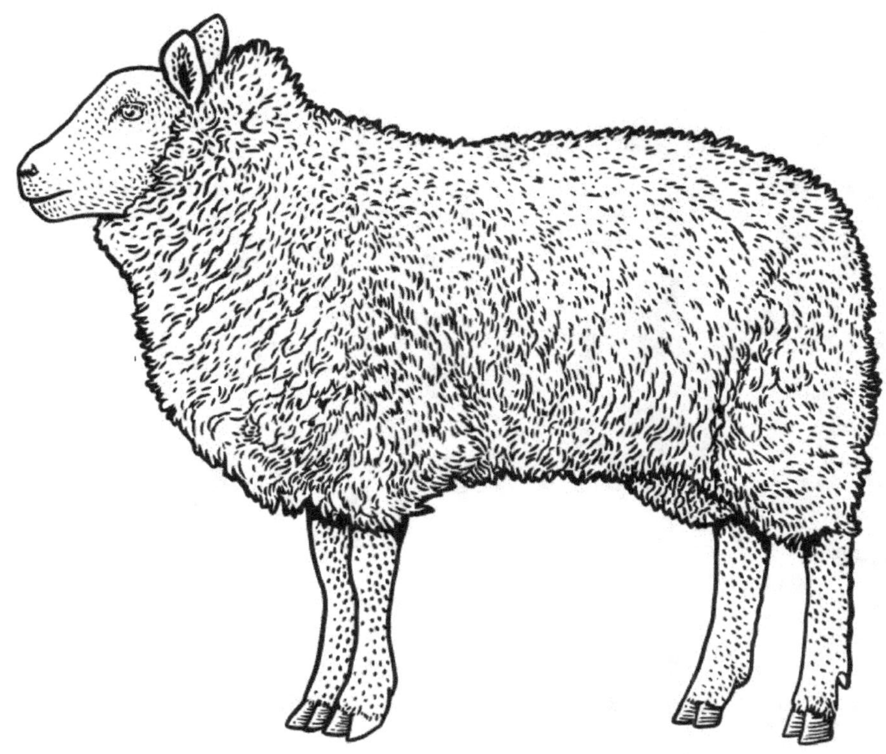

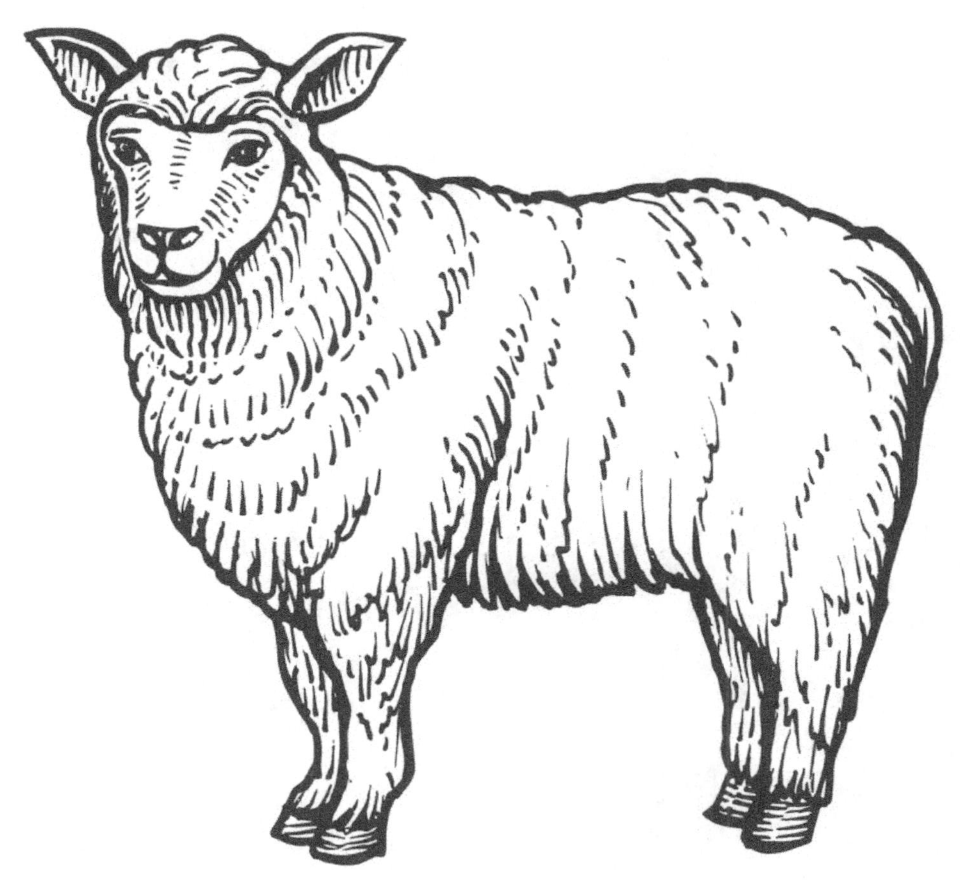

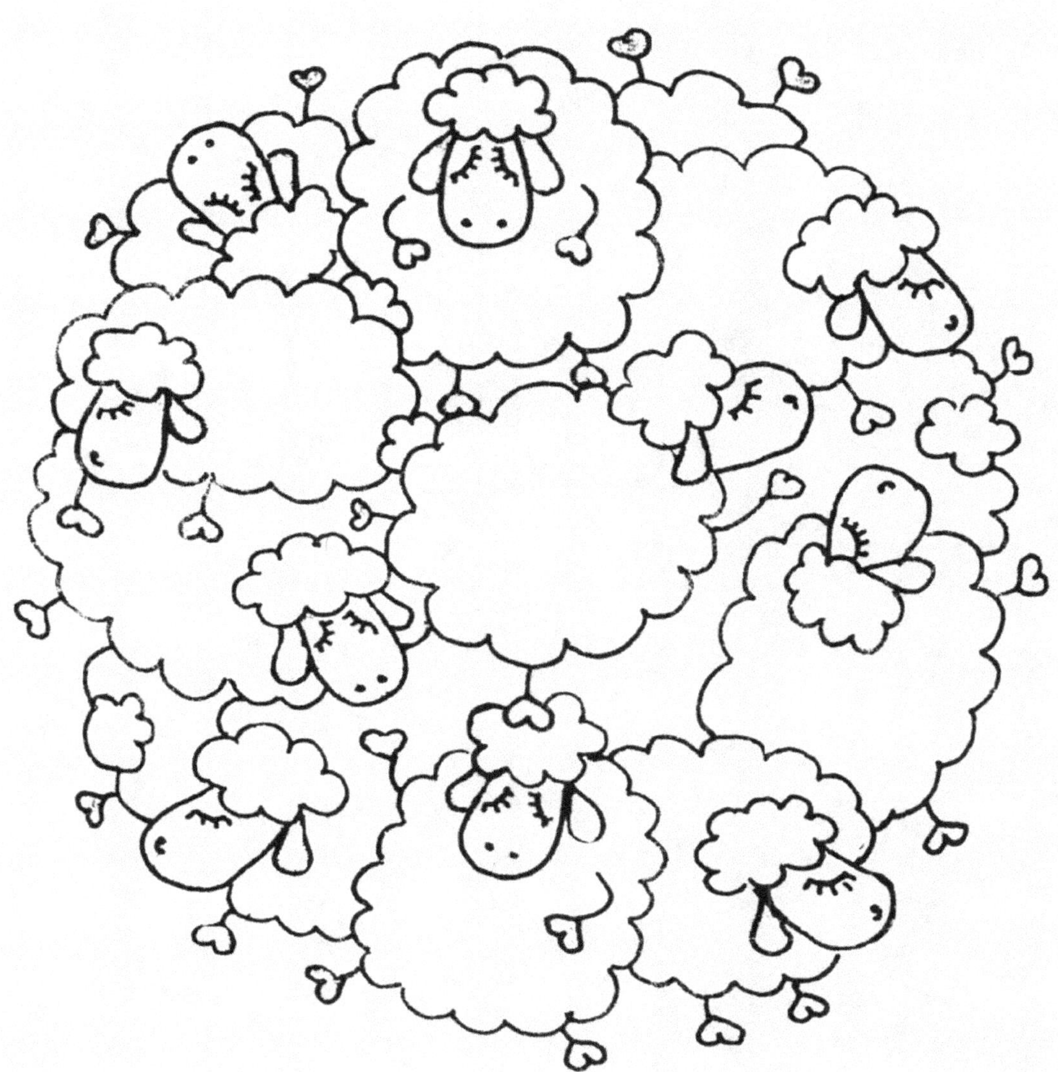

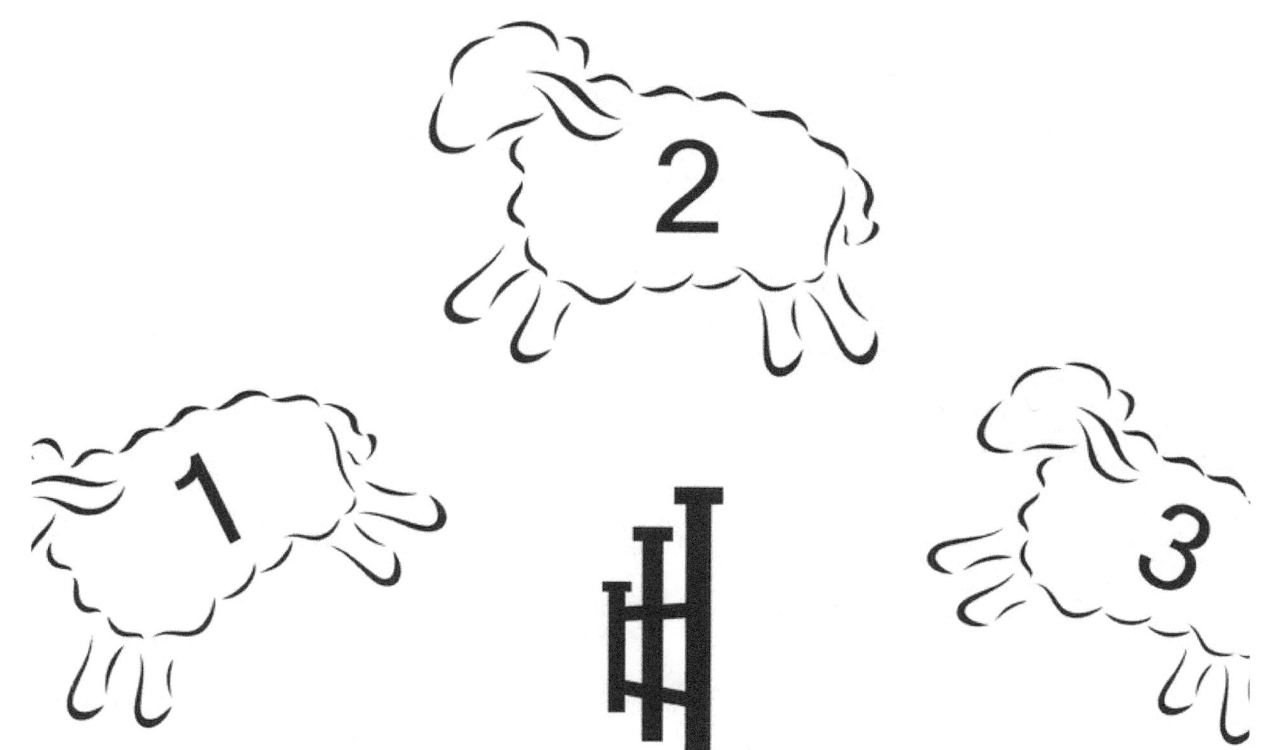

2
1
3

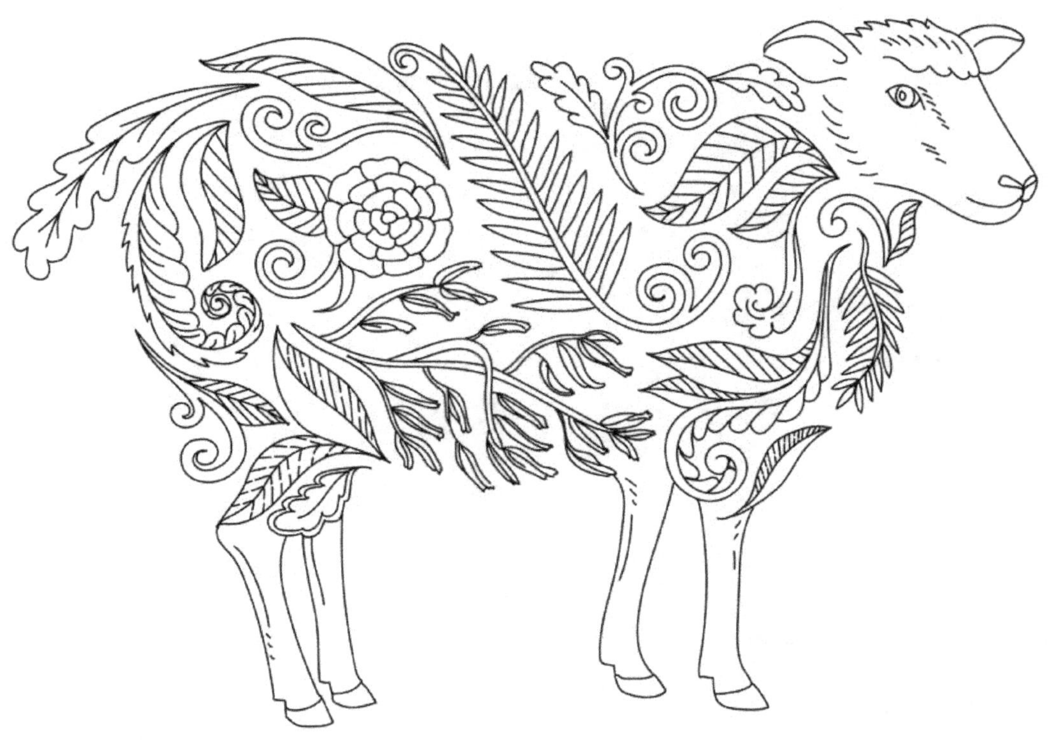

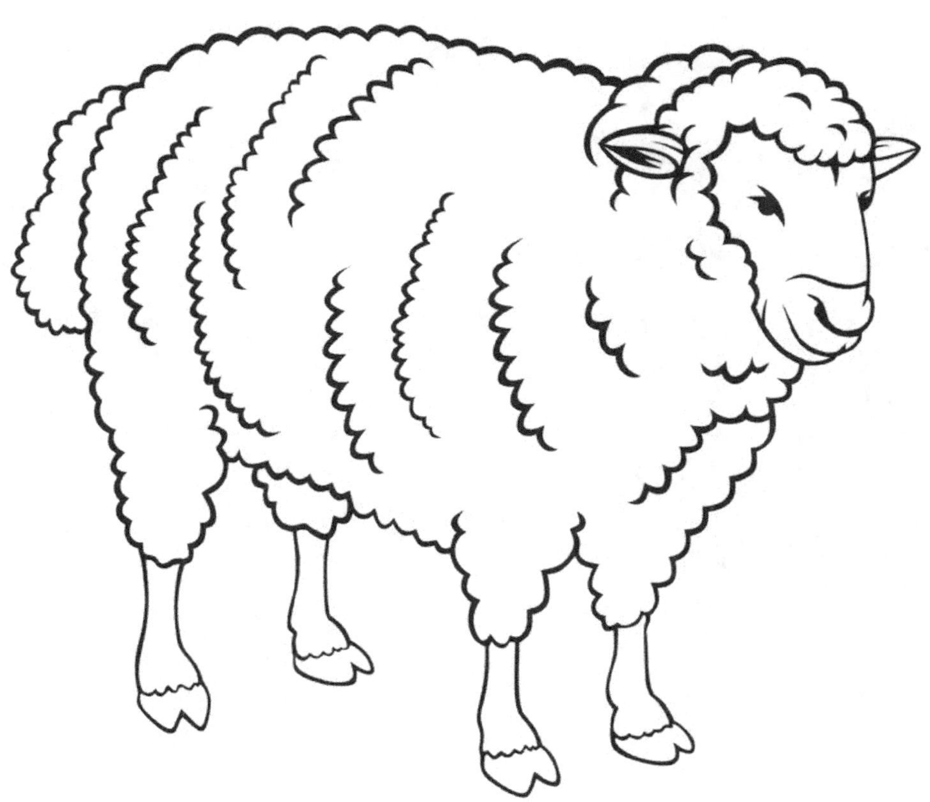

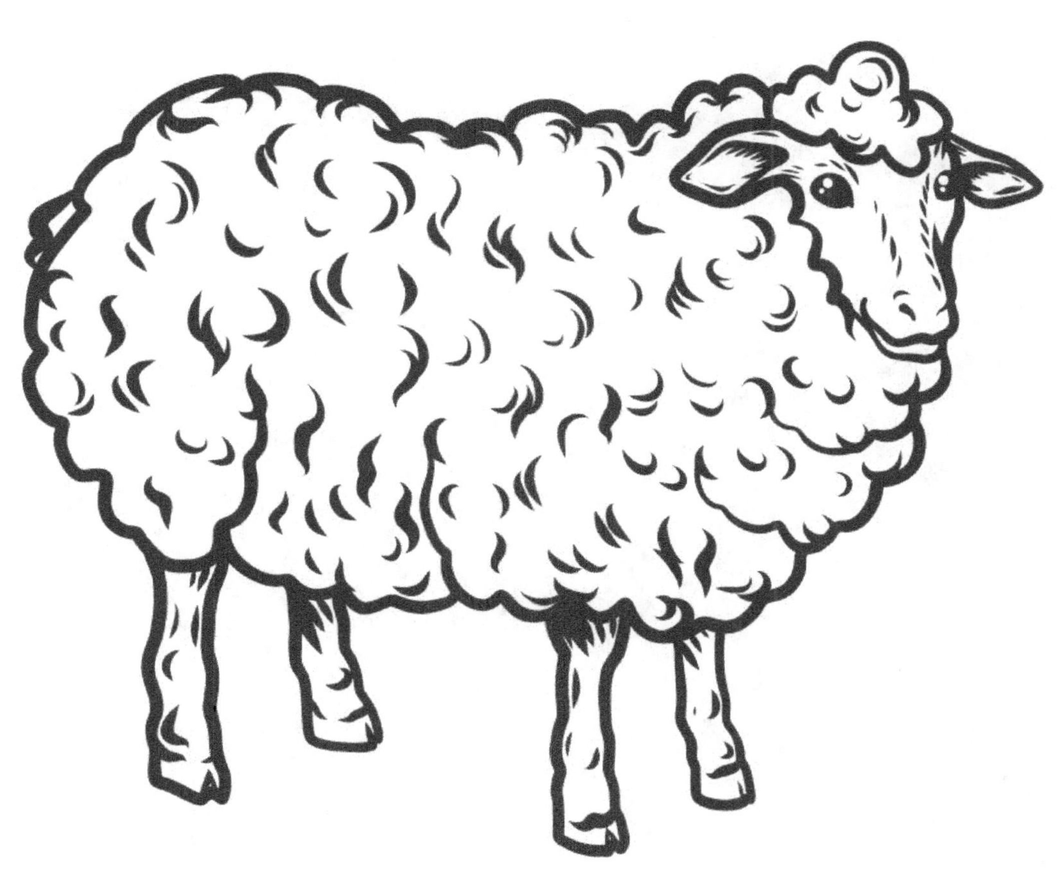

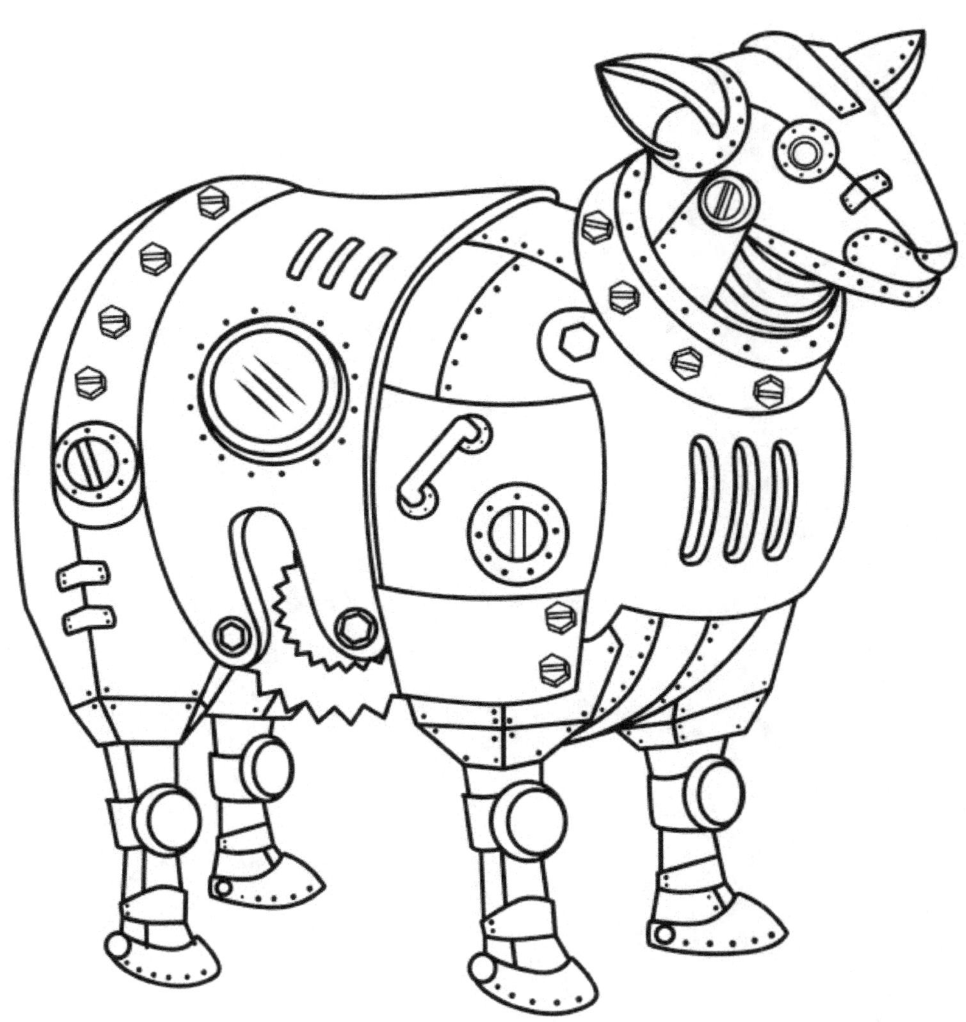

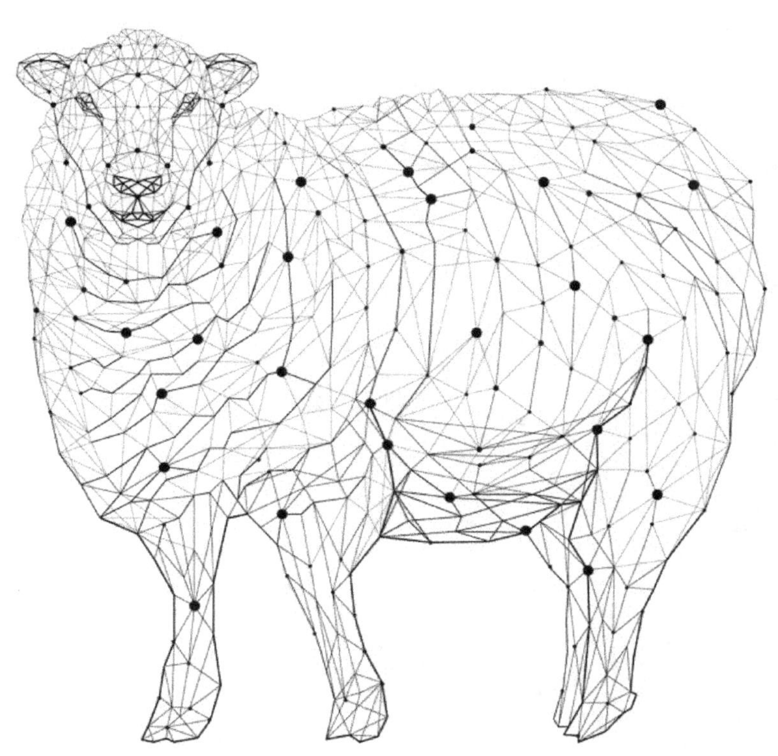

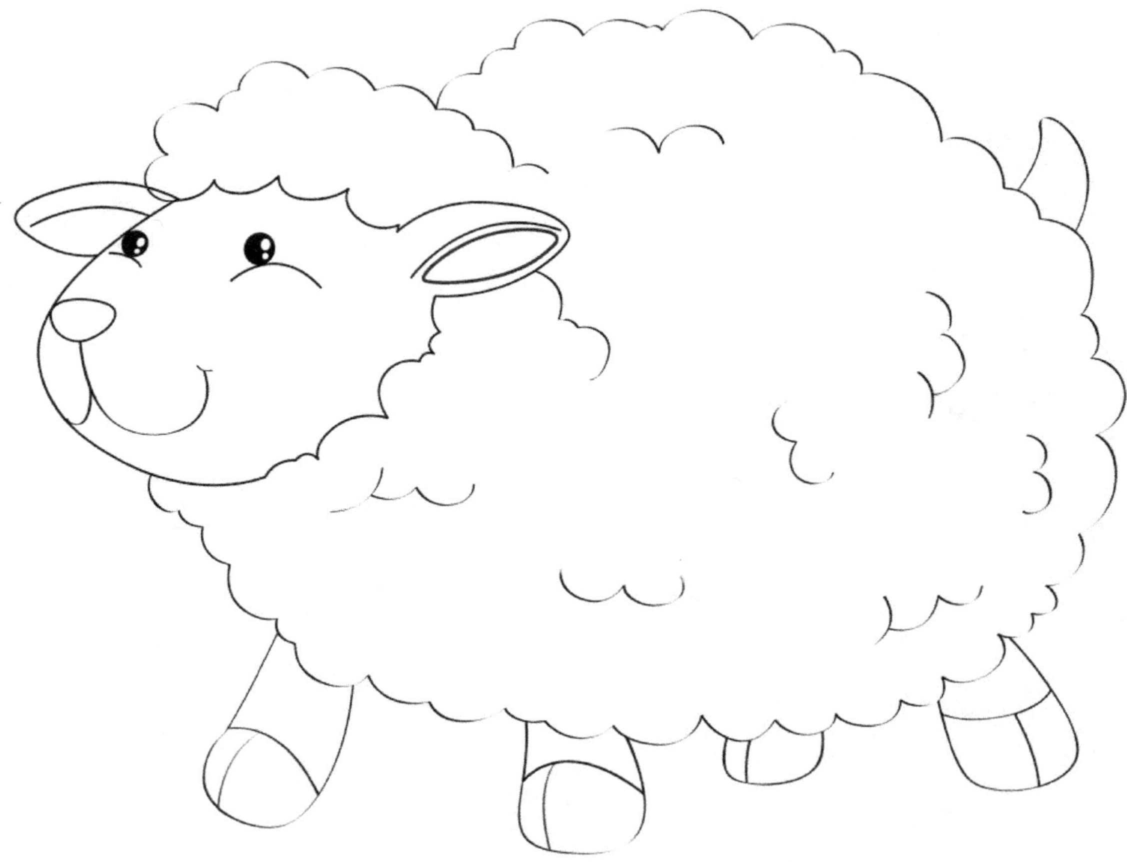

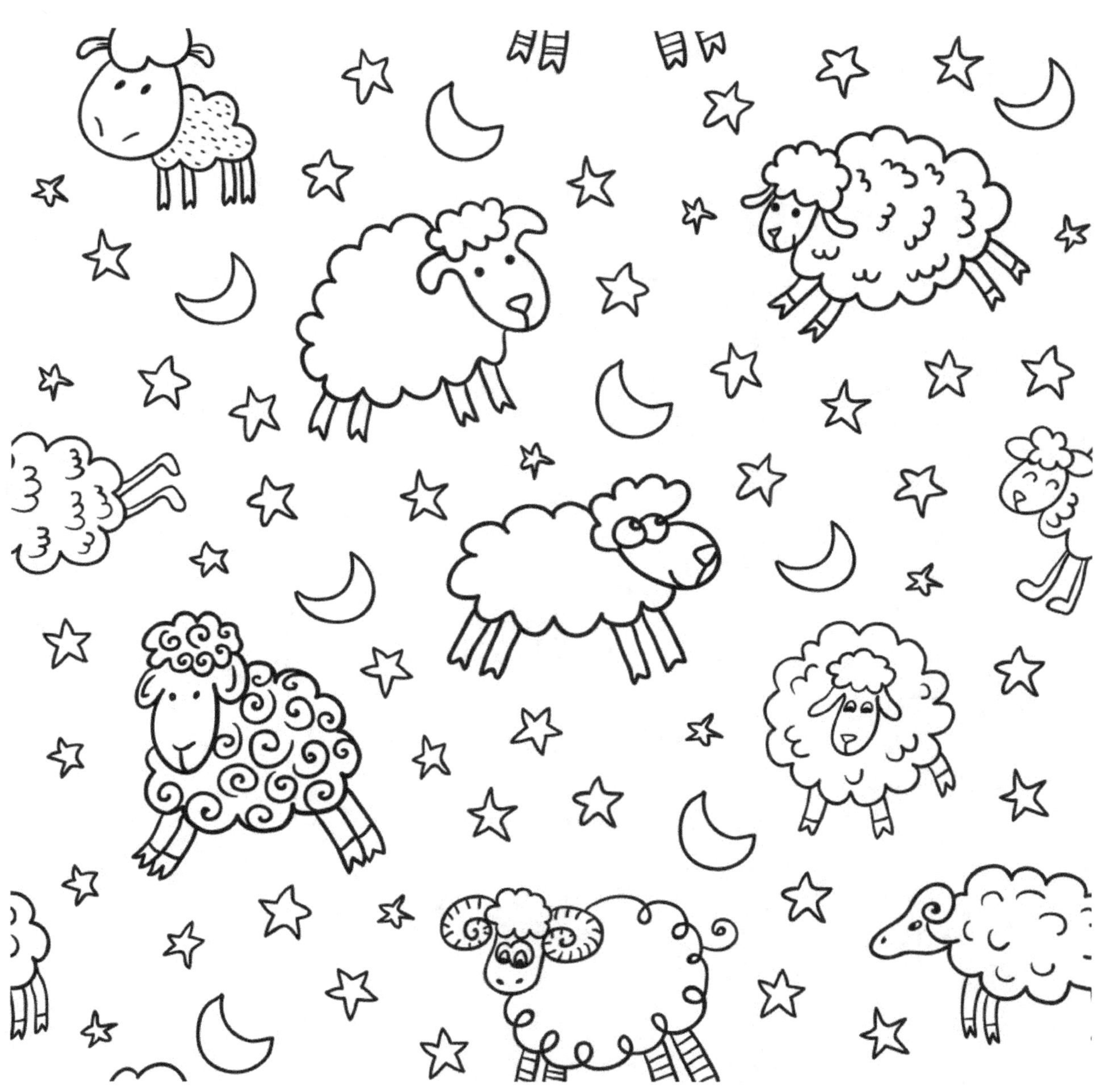